Dear Reader,
reviews and rating stars on Amazon are the lifeblood of
every independent author.
If you leave me a quick rating or review,
I'll deeply appreciate it and you will help me to buy my dogs more treats.
Thank you!

Impressum
Training4Paws
Pattbergstr. 15
74867 Neunkirchen
Germany

Copyright ©2020 by Training4Paws

SCENT DETECTION TRAINING LOG

DOG:
NAME:

AGE:

BREED:

TARGET SCENTS:

HEALTH ISSUES:

HANDLER:
NAME:

CONTACT:

TOP 5 FOOD REWARDS
_____
_____
_____
_____
_____

TOP 5 TOY REWARDS
_____
_____
_____
_____
_____

TOP 5 ENVIRONMENTAL REWARDS
_____
_____
_____
_____
_____

NOTES:

PROGRESS TRACKER

OVERALL EVALUATION

⭐☺ < 80%   ☺ 50 - 80%   ☹ > 50% SUCCESS RATE

DATE

YOU NAILED IT!
IT'S TIME TO UP CRITERIA!

KEEP TRAINING
AT THIS LEVEL

LOWER CRITERIA,
RETHINK YOUR TRAINING

DATE

YOU NAILED IT!
IT'S TIME TO UP CRITERIA!

KEEP TRAINING
AT THIS LEVEL

LOWER CRITERIA,
RETHINK YOUR TRAINING

PROGRESS TRACKER

OVERALL EVALUATION

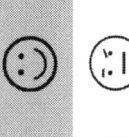

< 80%   50 - 80%   > 50% SUCCESS RATE

DATE

YOU NAILED IT!
IT'S TIME TO UP CRITERIA!

KEEP TRAINING
AT THIS LEVEL

LOWER CRITERIA,
RETHINK YOUR TRAINING

DATE

YOU NAILED IT!
IT'S TIME TO UP CRITERIA!

KEEP TRAINING
AT THIS LEVEL

LOWER CRITERIA,
RETHINK YOUR TRAINING

PROGRESS TRACKER

OVERALL EVALUATION

< 80%   50 - 80%   > 50% SUCCESS RATE

DATE

YOU NAILED IT!
IT'S TIME TO UP CRITERIA!

KEEP TRAINING
AT THIS LEVEL

LOWER CRITERIA,
RETHINK YOUR TRAINING

DATE

YOU NAILED IT!
IT'S TIME TO UP CRITERIA!

KEEP TRAINING
AT THIS LEVEL

LOWER CRITERIA,
RETHINK YOUR TRAINING

PROGRESS TRACKER

OVERALL EVALUATION

- ⭐ < 80%
- 🙂 50 – 80%
- 😕 > 50% SUCCESS RATE

DATE

YOU NAILED IT!
IT'S TIME TO UP CRITERIA!

KEEP TRAINING
AT THIS LEVEL

LOWER CRITERIA,
RETHINK YOUR TRAINING

DATE

YOU NAILED IT!
IT'S TIME TO UP CRITERIA!

KEEP TRAINING
AT THIS LEVEL

LOWER CRITERIA,
RETHINK YOUR TRAINING

SCENT DETECTION TRAINING NO.

LOCATION: **DATE:**

TARGET SCENT:

PRIORITIES
_____
_____
_____
_____
_____

SCENT ARTICLES:

HIDES:

NUMBER:

RESULTS
_____
_____
_____
_____

○ NOT CONTAMINATED
○ CONTAMINATED

SUCCESS:

NUMBER OF BLINDS:

NOTES
_____
_____
_____
_____
_____
_____
_____

SEARCH AREA:

HANDLER:

REWARD:

MOOD:

WEATHER CONDITIONS:

PROBLEMS:

OVERALL EVALUATION

⭐☆   🙂   😐

< 80%   50 - 80%   > 50% SUCCESS RATE

SCENT DETECTION TRAINING NO.

LOCATION: **DATE:**

TARGET SCENT:

PRIORITIES
_____
_____
_____
_____
_____

SCENT ARTICLES:

HIDES:
NUMBER:

RESULTS
_____
_____
_____
_____

○ NOT CONTAMINATED
○ CONTAMINATED

SUCCESS:

NUMBER OF BLINDS:

SEARCH AREA:

NOTES
_____
_____
_____
_____
_____
_____
_____
_____

HANDLER:
REWARD:

MOOD:

WEATHER CONDITIONS:

PROBLEMS:

OVERALL EVALUATION

☆☆   ☺   😐

< 80%   50 - 80%   > 50% SUCCESS RATE

SCENT DETECTION TRAINING NO.

LOCATION: **DATE:**

TARGET SCENT:

PRIORITIES

SCENT ARTICLES:

HIDES:

NUMBER:

RESULTS

○ NOT CONTAMINATED
○ CONTAMINATED

SUCCESS:

SEARCH AREA:

NUMBER OF BLINDS:

NOTES

HANDLER:

REWARD:

MOOD:

WEATHER CONDITIONS:

PROBLEMS:

OVERALL EVALUATION

☆☆ ☺ 😐

< 80%   50 – 80%   > 50% SUCCESS RATE

SCENT DETECTION TRAINING NO.

LOCATION: **DATE:**

TARGET SCENT:

PRIORITIES
_____
_____
_____
_____
_____

SCENT ARTICLES:

HIDES:

NUMBER:

RESULTS
_____
_____
_____
_____
_____

○ NOT CONTAMINATED
○ CONTAMINATED

SUCCESS:

NUMBER OF BLINDS:

SEARCH AREA:

NOTES
_____
_____
_____
_____
_____
_____
_____
_____

HANDLER:

REWARD:

MOOD:

WEATHER CONDITIONS:

PROBLEMS:

OVERALL EVALUATION

😎   🙂   😐

< 80%   50 - 80%   > 50% SUCCESS RATE

SCENT DETECTION TRAINING NO.

LOCATION: **DATE:**

TARGET SCENT:

HIDES:
NUMBER:

SUCCESS:

NUMBER OF BLINDS:

HANDLER:
REWARD:

MOOD:

PROBLEMS:

PRIORITIES

RESULTS

NOTES

SCENT ARTICLES:

○ NOT CONTAMINATED
○ CONTAMINATED

SEARCH AREA:

WEATHER CONDITIONS:

OVERALL EVALUATION

☆☺☆   ☺   😐

< 80%   50 - 80%   > 50% SUCCESS RATE

SCENT DETECTION TRAINING NO.

LOCATION: **DATE:**

TARGET SCENT:

PRIORITIES
_____
_____
_____
_____
_____

SCENT ARTICLES:

○ NOT CONTAMINATED
○ CONTAMINATED

HIDES:
NUMBER:

RESULTS
_____
_____
_____
_____

SUCCESS:

NUMBER OF BLINDS:

SEARCH AREA:

NOTES
_____
_____
_____
_____

HANDLER:
REWARD:

WEATHER CONDITIONS:

MOOD:

_____
_____
_____

PROBLEMS:

OVERALL EVALUATION

⭐☺   ☺   😠

< 80%   50 - 80%   > 50% SUCCESS RATE

SCENT DETECTION TRAINING NO.

LOCATION: **DATE:**

TARGET SCENT:

PRIORITIES

SCENT ARTICLES:

HIDES:
NUMBER:

RESULTS

○ NOT CONTAMINATED
○ CONTAMINATED

SUCCESS:

NUMBER OF BLINDS:

SEARCH AREA:

NOTES

HANDLER:
REWARD:

MOOD:

WEATHER CONDITIONS:

PROBLEMS:

OVERALL EVALUATION

< 80%   50 - 80%   > 50% SUCCESS RATE

SCENT DETECTION TRAINING NO.

LOCATION: **DATE:**

TARGET SCENT:

PRIORITIES
_____
_____
_____
_____

SCENT ARTICLES:

HIDES:

NUMBER:

RESULTS
_____
_____
_____
_____

○ NOT CONTAMINATED
○ CONTAMINATED

SUCCESS:

NUMBER OF BLINDS:

SEARCH AREA:

NOTES
_____
_____
_____
_____
_____
_____
_____

HANDLER:

REWARD:

MOOD:

WEATHER CONDITIONS:

PROBLEMS:

OVERALL EVALUATION

⭐☆   ☺   😐

< 80%   50 - 80%   > 50% SUCCESS RATE

SCENT DETECTION TRAINING NO.

LOCATION: **DATE:**

TARGET SCENT:

PRIORITIES
_____
_____
_____
_____
_____

SCENT ARTICLES:

○ NOT CONTAMINATED
○ CONTAMINATED

HIDES:

NUMBER:

SUCCESS:

NUMBER OF BLINDS:

RESULTS
_____
_____
_____
_____
_____

SEARCH AREA:

NOTES
_____
_____
_____
_____
_____
_____
_____

HANDLER:

REWARD:

MOOD:

PROBLEMS:

WEATHER CONDITIONS:

OVERALL EVALUATION

⭐⭐   ☺   😐

< 80%   50 – 80%   > 50% SUCCESS RATE

SCENT DETECTION TRAINING NO.

LOCATION: **DATE:**

TARGET SCENT:

PRIORITIES
_____
_____
_____
_____

SCENT ARTICLES:

HIDES:
NUMBER:

RESULTS
_____
_____

○ NOT CONTAMINATED
○ CONTAMINATED

SUCCESS:
_____
_____

NUMBER OF BLINDS:

SEARCH AREA:

NOTES
_____

HANDLER:
REWARD:
_____
_____
_____

MOOD:
_____
_____

WEATHER CONDITIONS:

PROBLEMS:

OVERALL EVALUATION

☆☺   ☺   😐

< 80%   50 - 80%   > 50% SUCCESS RATE

SCENT DETECTION TRAINING NO.

LOCATION: **DATE:**

TARGET SCENT:

PRIORITIES
_____
_____
_____
_____
_____

SCENT ARTICLES:

HIDES:

NUMBER:

RESULTS
_____
_____
_____
_____
_____

○ NOT CONTAMINATED
○ CONTAMINATED

SUCCESS:

NUMBER OF BLINDS:

SEARCH AREA:

NOTES
_____
_____
_____
_____

HANDLER:

REWARD:

_____
_____
_____
_____

WEATHER CONDITIONS:

MOOD:

PROBLEMS:

OVERALL EVALUATION

⭐ 😊 😐
< 80%   50 - 80%   > 50% SUCCESS RATE

SCENT DETECTION TRAINING NO.

LOCATION: **DATE:**

TARGET SCENT:

PRIORITIES

SCENT ARTICLES:

HIDES:
NUMBER:

RESULTS

○ NOT CONTAMINATED
○ CONTAMINATED

SUCCESS:

SEARCH AREA:

NUMBER OF BLINDS:

NOTES

HANDLER:
REWARD:

MOOD:

WEATHER CONDITIONS:

PROBLEMS:

OVERALL EVALUATION

< 80%   50 - 80%   > 50% SUCCESS RATE

SCENT DETECTION TRAINING NO.

LOCATION: **DATE:**

TARGET SCENT:

PRIORITIES
_____
_____
_____
_____
_____

SCENT ARTICLES:

HIDES:

NUMBER:

RESULTS
_____
_____
_____
_____

○ NOT CONTAMINATED
○ CONTAMINATED

SUCCESS:

NUMBER OF BLINDS:

SEARCH AREA:

NOTES
_____
_____
_____
_____
_____
_____
_____
_____
_____

HANDLER:

REWARD:

MOOD:

WEATHER CONDITIONS:

PROBLEMS:

OVERALL EVALUATION

⭐☺   ☺   😐

< 80%   50 - 80%   > 50% SUCCESS RATE

SCENT DETECTION TRAINING NO.

LOCATION: **DATE:**

TARGET SCENT:

PRIORITIES

SCENT ARTICLES:

HIDES:
NUMBER:

RESULTS

○ NOT CONTAMINATED
○ CONTAMINATED

SUCCESS:

SEARCH AREA:

NUMBER OF BLINDS:

NOTES

HANDLER:
REWARD:

MOOD:

WEATHER CONDITIONS:

PROBLEMS:

OVERALL EVALUATION

⭐☺ ☺ 😐
< 80% 50 - 80% > 50% SUCCESS RATE

SCENT DETECTION TRAINING NO.

LOCATION: **DATE:**

TARGET SCENT:

PRIORITIES
_____
_____
_____
_____
_____

SCENT ARTICLES:

HIDES:

NUMBER:

RESULTS
_____
_____
_____

○ NOT CONTAMINATED
○ CONTAMINATED

SUCCESS:

NUMBER OF BLINDS:

SEARCH AREA:

NOTES
_____
_____
_____
_____
_____
_____
_____
_____

HANDLER:

REWARD:

WEATHER CONDITIONS:

MOOD:

PROBLEMS:

OVERALL EVALUATION

⭐☆   ☺   😐

< 80%   50 - 80%   > 50% SUCCESS RATE

SCENT DETECTION TRAINING NO.

LOCATION: **DATE:**

TARGET SCENT:

PRIORITIES

SCENT ARTICLES:

HIDES:
NUMBER:

RESULTS

○ NOT CONTAMINATED
○ CONTAMINATED

SUCCESS:

NUMBER OF BLINDS:

SEARCH AREA:

NOTES

HANDLER:
REWARD:

MOOD:

WEATHER CONDITIONS:

PROBLEMS:

OVERALL EVALUATION

☆☆   ☺   😐

< 80%   50 - 80%   > 50% SUCCESS RATE

SCENT DETECTION TRAINING NO.

LOCATION: **DATE:**

TARGET SCENT:

PRIORITIES

SCENT ARTICLES:

HIDES:

NUMBER:

RESULTS

○ NOT CONTAMINATED
○ CONTAMINATED

SUCCESS:

NUMBER OF BLINDS:

SEARCH AREA:

NOTES

HANDLER:

REWARD:

MOOD:

WEATHER CONDITIONS:

PROBLEMS:

OVERALL EVALUATION

☆☆   ☺   😒

< 80%   50 - 80%   > 50% SUCCESS RATE

SCENT DETECTION TRAINING NO.

LOCATION: **DATE:**

TARGET SCENT:

PRIORITIES
_____
_____
_____
_____
_____

SCENT ARTICLES:

HIDES:

NUMBER:

RESULTS
_____
_____
_____
_____
_____

○ NOT CONTAMINATED
○ CONTAMINATED

SUCCESS:

NUMBER OF BLINDS:

SEARCH AREA:

NOTES
_____
_____
_____
_____
_____
_____
_____
_____
_____

HANDLER:

REWARD:

MOOD:

WEATHER CONDITIONS:

PROBLEMS:

OVERALL EVALUATION

☆☺   ☺   😐

< 80%   50 - 80%   > 50% SUCCESS RATE

SCENT DETECTION TRAINING NO.

LOCATION: **DATE:**

TARGET SCENT:

PRIORITIES

SCENT ARTICLES:

HIDES:
NUMBER:

RESULTS

○ NOT CONTAMINATED
○ CONTAMINATED

SUCCESS:

NUMBER OF BLINDS:

SEARCH AREA:

NOTES

HANDLER:
REWARD:

MOOD:

WEATHER CONDITIONS:

PROBLEMS:

OVERALL EVALUATION

☆☆ ☺ 😐
< 80%   50 - 80%   > 50% SUCCESS RATE

SCENT DETECTION TRAINING NO.

LOCATION: **DATE:**

TARGET SCENT:

HIDES:

NUMBER:

SUCCESS:

NUMBER OF BLINDS:

HANDLER:

REWARD:

MOOD:

PROBLEMS:

PRIORITIES

RESULTS

NOTES

OVERALL EVALUATION

☆☺   ☺   😐

< 80%   50 - 80%   > 50% SUCCESS RATE

SCENT ARTICLES:

○ NOT CONTAMINATED
○ CONTAMINATED

SEARCH AREA:

WEATHER CONDITIONS:

SCENT DETECTION TRAINING NO.

LOCATION: **DATE:**

TARGET SCENT:

PRIORITIES

SCENT ARTICLES:

HIDES:

NUMBER:

RESULTS

○ NOT CONTAMINATED
○ CONTAMINATED

SUCCESS:

NUMBER OF BLINDS:

SEARCH AREA:

NOTES

HANDLER:

REWARD:

MOOD:

WEATHER CONDITIONS:

PROBLEMS:

OVERALL EVALUATION

☆☆   ☺   😐

< 80%   50 - 80%   > 50% SUCCESS RATE

SCENT DETECTION TRAINING NO.

LOCATION: **DATE:**

TARGET SCENT:

PRIORITIES
_____
_____
_____
_____
_____

SCENT ARTICLES:

HIDES:
NUMBER:

RESULTS
_____
_____
_____
_____

○ NOT CONTAMINATED
○ CONTAMINATED

SUCCESS:

NUMBER OF BLINDS:

NOTES
_____
_____
_____
_____
_____
_____
_____
_____

SEARCH AREA:

HANDLER:
REWARD:

MOOD:

WEATHER CONDITIONS:

PROBLEMS:

OVERALL EVALUATION

☆☆   ☺   😐

< 80%   50 - 80%   > 50% SUCCESS RATE

SCENT DETECTION TRAINING NO.

LOCATION: **DATE:**

TARGET SCENT:

PRIORITIES
_____
_____
_____
_____
_____

SCENT ARTICLES:

HIDES:

NUMBER:

RESULTS
_____
_____
_____
_____
_____

○ NOT CONTAMINATED
○ CONTAMINATED

SUCCESS:

NUMBER OF BLINDS:

SEARCH AREA:

NOTES
_____
_____
_____
_____
_____
_____
_____
_____
_____

HANDLER:

REWARD:

MOOD:

WEATHER CONDITIONS:

PROBLEMS:

OVERALL EVALUATION

☆☆ ☺ 😐
< 80%   50 – 80%   > 50% SUCCESS RATE

SCENT DETECTION TRAINING NO.

LOCATION: **DATE:**

TARGET SCENT:

PRIORITIES
_____
_____
_____
_____

SCENT ARTICLES:

○ NOT CONTAMINATED
○ CONTAMINATED

HIDES:
NUMBER:

RESULTS
_____
_____
_____
_____

SUCCESS:

SEARCH AREA:

NUMBER OF BLINDS:

NOTES
_____
_____
_____
_____
_____
_____
_____
_____

HANDLER:
REWARD:

MOOD:

WEATHER CONDITIONS:

PROBLEMS:

OVERALL EVALUATION

☆☺ ☺ 😐
< 80%   50 - 80%   > 50% SUCCESS RATE

SCENT DETECTION TRAINING NO.

LOCATION: **DATE:**

TARGET SCENT:

PRIORITIES
_____
_____
_____
_____
_____

SCENT ARTICLES:

HIDES:
NUMBER:

RESULTS
_____
_____
_____
_____

○ NOT CONTAMINATED
○ CONTAMINATED

SUCCESS:

NUMBER OF BLINDS:

NOTES
_____
_____
_____
_____
_____
_____
_____
_____
_____
_____

SEARCH AREA:

HANDLER:
REWARD:

MOOD:

WEATHER CONDITIONS:

PROBLEMS:

OVERALL EVALUATION

☆☆   ☺   😐

< 80%   50 – 80%   > 50% SUCCESS RATE

SCENT DETECTION TRAINING NO.

LOCATION: **DATE:**

TARGET SCENT:

HIDES:

NUMBER:

SUCCESS:

NUMBER OF BLINDS:

HANDLER:

REWARD:

MOOD:

PROBLEMS:

PRIORITIES

RESULTS

NOTES

OVERALL EVALUATION

○ ☆☆   ○ ☺   ○ 😐

< 80%   50 – 80%   > 50% SUCCESS RATE

SCENT ARTICLES:

○ NOT CONTAMINATED
○ CONTAMINATED

SEARCH AREA:

WEATHER CONDITIONS:

SCENT DETECTION TRAINING NO.

LOCATION: **DATE:**

TARGET SCENT:

PRIORITIES

SCENT ARTICLES:

HIDES:
NUMBER:

RESULTS

○ NOT CONTAMINATED
○ CONTAMINATED

SUCCESS:

NUMBER OF BLINDS:

SEARCH AREA:

NOTES

HANDLER:
REWARD:

MOOD:

WEATHER CONDITIONS:

PROBLEMS:

OVERALL EVALUATION

☆☆   ☺   😐
< 80%   50 - 80%   > 50% SUCCESS RATE

SCENT DETECTION TRAINING NO.

LOCATION: **DATE:**

TARGET SCENT:

HIDES:
NUMBER:

SUCCESS:

NUMBER OF BLINDS:

HANDLER:
REWARD:

MOOD:

PROBLEMS:

PRIORITIES

RESULTS

NOTES

OVERALL EVALUATION

< 80%   50 - 80%   > 50% SUCCESS RATE

SCENT ARTICLES:

○ NOT CONTAMINATED
○ CONTAMINATED

SEARCH AREA:

WEATHER CONDITIONS:

SCENT DETECTION TRAINING NO.

LOCATION: **DATE:**

TARGET SCENT:

PRIORITIES
_____
_____
_____
_____
_____

SCENT ARTICLES:

HIDES:

NUMBER:

RESULTS
_____
_____
_____
_____

○ NOT CONTAMINATED
○ CONTAMINATED

SUCCESS:

NUMBER OF BLINDS:

SEARCH AREA:

NOTES
_____
_____
_____
_____

HANDLER:

REWARD:

_____
_____
_____
_____

MOOD:

WEATHER CONDITIONS:

PROBLEMS:

OVERALL EVALUATION

⭐ 😊 😐

< 80%   50 – 80%   > 50% SUCCESS RATE

SCENT DETECTION TRAINING NO.

LOCATION: **DATE:**

TARGET SCENT:

HIDES:
NUMBER:

SUCCESS:

NUMBER OF BLINDS:

HANDLER:
REWARD:

MOOD:

PROBLEMS:

PRIORITIES
_____
_____
_____
_____
_____

RESULTS
_____
_____
_____
_____

NOTES
_____
_____
_____
_____
_____
_____
_____
_____

OVERALL EVALUATION

☆☆ 🙂   🙂   😐

< 80%   50 - 80%   > 50% SUCCESS RATE

SCENT ARTICLES:

◯ NOT CONTAMINATED
◯ CONTAMINATED

SEARCH AREA:

WEATHER CONDITIONS:

SCENT DETECTION TRAINING NO.

LOCATION: **DATE:**

TARGET SCENT:

PRIORITIES
_____
_____
_____
_____

SCENT ARTICLES:

HIDES:
NUMBER:

RESULTS
_____
_____

○ NOT CONTAMINATED
○ CONTAMINATED

SUCCESS:

_____
_____

NUMBER OF BLINDS:

NOTES
_____

SEARCH AREA:

HANDLER:
REWARD:

_____
_____
_____
_____
_____
_____

MOOD:

WEATHER CONDITIONS:

_____
_____

PROBLEMS:

OVERALL EVALUATION

☆☺   ☺   😒

< 80%   50 - 80%   > 50% SUCCESS RATE

SCENT DETECTION TRAINING NO.

LOCATION: **DATE:**

TARGET SCENT:

HIDES:
NUMBER:
SUCCESS:
NUMBER OF BLINDS:

HANDLER:
REWARD:
MOOD:
PROBLEMS:

PRIORITIES
_____
_____
_____
_____
_____

RESULTS
_____
_____
_____
_____

NOTES
_____
_____
_____
_____
_____
_____
_____

OVERALL EVALUATION

☆☺ ☺ 😐
< 80%   50 - 80%   > 50% SUCCESS RATE

SCENT ARTICLES:

○ NOT CONTAMINATED
○ CONTAMINATED

SEARCH AREA:

WEATHER CONDITIONS:

SCENT DETECTION TRAINING NO.

LOCATION: **DATE:**

TARGET SCENT:

PRIORITIES

SCENT ARTICLES:

HIDES:
NUMBER:

RESULTS

○ NOT CONTAMINATED
○ CONTAMINATED

SUCCESS:

NUMBER OF BLINDS:

SEARCH AREA:

NOTES

HANDLER:
REWARD:

MOOD:

WEATHER CONDITIONS:

PROBLEMS:

OVERALL EVALUATION

☆☆ ☺ 😒
< 80%   50 - 80%   > 50% SUCCESS RATE

SCENT DETECTION TRAINING NO.

LOCATION: **DATE:**

TARGET SCENT:

PRIORITIES
_____
_____
_____
_____

SCENT ARTICLES:

HIDES:
NUMBER:

RESULTS
_____
_____
_____
_____

○ NOT CONTAMINATED
○ CONTAMINATED

SUCCESS:

NUMBER OF BLINDS:

NOTES
_____
_____
_____
_____
_____
_____
_____
_____

SEARCH AREA:

HANDLER:
REWARD:

MOOD:

WEATHER CONDITIONS:

PROBLEMS:

OVERALL EVALUATION

⭐☺   ☺   😐
< 80%   50 - 80%   > 50% SUCCESS RATE

SCENT DETECTION TRAINING NO.

LOCATION: **DATE:**

TARGET SCENT:

PRIORITIES

SCENT ARTICLES:

HIDES:

NUMBER:

RESULTS

○ NOT CONTAMINATED
○ CONTAMINATED

SUCCESS:

NUMBER OF BLINDS:

SEARCH AREA:

NOTES

HANDLER:

REWARD:

MOOD:

WEATHER CONDITIONS:

PROBLEMS:

OVERALL EVALUATION

☆☆   ☺   😐
< 80%   50 - 80%   > 50% SUCCESS RATE

SCENT DETECTION TRAINING NO.

LOCATION: **DATE:**

TARGET SCENT:

HIDES:
NUMBER:
SUCCESS:
NUMBER OF BLINDS:

HANDLER:
REWARD:
MOOD:
PROBLEMS:

PRIORITIES

RESULTS

NOTES

OVERALL EVALUATION

< 80%   50 - 80%   > 50% SUCCESS RATE

SCENT ARTICLES:

○ NOT CONTAMINATED
○ CONTAMINATED

SEARCH AREA:

WEATHER CONDITIONS:

SCENT DETECTION TRAINING NO.

LOCATION: **DATE:**

TARGET SCENT:

PRIORITIES

SCENT ARTICLES:

HIDES:
NUMBER:

RESULTS

○ NOT CONTAMINATED
○ CONTAMINATED

SUCCESS:

NUMBER OF BLINDS:

SEARCH AREA:

NOTES

HANDLER:
REWARD:

MOOD:

WEATHER CONDITIONS:

PROBLEMS:

OVERALL EVALUATION

☆☆   ☺   😐
< 80%   50 - 80%   > 50% SUCCESS RATE

SCENT DETECTION TRAINING NO.

LOCATION: **DATE:**

TARGET SCENT:

PRIORITIES

SCENT ARTICLES:

HIDES:
NUMBER:

RESULTS

○ NOT CONTAMINATED
○ CONTAMINATED

SUCCESS:

NUMBER OF BLINDS:

SEARCH AREA:

NOTES

HANDLER:
REWARD:

WEATHER CONDITIONS:

MOOD:

PROBLEMS:

OVERALL EVALUATION

☆☆ ☺ 😐

< 80%   50 - 80%   > 50% SUCCESS RATE

SCENT DETECTION TRAINING NO.

LOCATION: **DATE:**

TARGET SCENT:

PRIORITIES

SCENT ARTICLES:

HIDES:
NUMBER:

RESULTS

○ NOT CONTAMINATED
○ CONTAMINATED

SUCCESS:

NUMBER OF BLINDS:

SEARCH AREA:

NOTES

HANDLER:
REWARD:

MOOD:

WEATHER CONDITIONS:

PROBLEMS:

OVERALL EVALUATION

< 80% 50 - 80% > 50% SUCCESS RATE

SCENT DETECTION TRAINING NO.

LOCATION: **DATE:**

TARGET SCENT:

PRIORITIES
_____
_____
_____
_____
_____

SCENT ARTICLES:

HIDES:

NUMBER:

RESULTS
_____
_____
_____
_____
_____

○ NOT CONTAMINATED
○ CONTAMINATED

SUCCESS:

NUMBER OF BLINDS:

SEARCH AREA:

NOTES
_____
_____
_____
_____

HANDLER:

REWARD:

_____
_____
_____
_____

WEATHER CONDITIONS:

MOOD:

PROBLEMS:

OVERALL EVALUATION

⭐☺   ☺   😐

< 80%   50 - 80%   > 50% SUCCESS RATE

SCENT DETECTION TRAINING NO.

LOCATION: **DATE:**

TARGET SCENT:

PRIORITIES

SCENT ARTICLES:

HIDES:
NUMBER:

RESULTS

○ NOT CONTAMINATED
○ CONTAMINATED

SUCCESS:

NUMBER OF BLINDS:

SEARCH AREA:

NOTES

HANDLER:
REWARD:

WEATHER CONDITIONS:

MOOD:

PROBLEMS:

OVERALL EVALUATION

☆☆ ☺ 😠
< 80%   50 - 80%   > 50% SUCCESS RATE

SCENT DETECTION TRAINING NO.

LOCATION: **DATE:**

TARGET SCENT:

PRIORITIES

SCENT ARTICLES:

HIDES:
NUMBER:

RESULTS

◯ NOT CONTAMINATED
◯ CONTAMINATED

SUCCESS:

SEARCH AREA:

NUMBER OF BLINDS:

NOTES

HANDLER:
REWARD:

MOOD:

WEATHER CONDITIONS:

PROBLEMS:

OVERALL EVALUATION

< 80% | 50 - 80% | > 50% SUCCESS RATE

SCENT DETECTION TRAINING NO.

LOCATION: **DATE:**

TARGET SCENT:

PRIORITIES

SCENT ARTICLES:

○ NOT CONTAMINATED
○ CONTAMINATED

HIDES:
NUMBER:

RESULTS

SUCCESS:

NUMBER OF BLINDS:

SEARCH AREA:

NOTES

HANDLER:
REWARD:

MOOD:

WEATHER CONDITIONS:

PROBLEMS:

OVERALL EVALUATION

⭐ ☺ 😐

< 80%   50 - 80%   > 50% SUCCESS RATE

SCENT DETECTION TRAINING NO.

LOCATION:　　　　　　　　　　DATE:

TARGET SCENT:

PRIORITIES

SCENT ARTICLES:

HIDES:
NUMBER:

RESULTS

○ NOT CONTAMINATED
○ CONTAMINATED

SUCCESS:

NUMBER OF BLINDS:

SEARCH AREA:

NOTES

HANDLER:
REWARD:

MOOD:

WEATHER CONDITIONS:

PROBLEMS:

OVERALL EVALUATION

☺☆　　　☺　　　😐
< 80%　　50 - 80%　　> 50% SUCCESS RATE

SCENT DETECTION TRAINING NO.

LOCATION: **DATE:**

TARGET SCENT:

HIDES:

NUMBER:

SUCCESS:

NUMBER OF BLINDS:

HANDLER:

REWARD:

MOOD:

PROBLEMS:

PRIORITIES

RESULTS

NOTES

OVERALL EVALUATION

☆☆   ☺   😒

< 80%   50 - 80%   > 50% SUCCESS RATE

SCENT ARTICLES:

○ NOT CONTAMINATED
○ CONTAMINATED

SEARCH AREA:

WEATHER CONDITIONS:

SCENT DETECTION TRAINING NO.

LOCATION: **DATE:**

TARGET SCENT:

HIDES:
NUMBER:

SUCCESS:

NUMBER OF BLINDS:

HANDLER:
REWARD:

MOOD:

PROBLEMS:

PRIORITIES

RESULTS

NOTES

SCENT ARTICLES:

◯ NOT CONTAMINATED
◯ CONTAMINATED

SEARCH AREA:

WEATHER CONDITIONS:

OVERALL EVALUATION

☆☆   ☺   😐

< 80%   50 – 80%   > 50% SUCCESS RATE

SCENT DETECTION TRAINING NO.

LOCATION: **DATE:**

TARGET SCENT:

PRIORITIES
_____
_____
_____
_____
_____

SCENT ARTICLES:

HIDES:
NUMBER:

RESULTS
_____
_____
_____
_____
_____

○ NOT CONTAMINATED
○ CONTAMINATED

SUCCESS:

NUMBER OF BLINDS:

SEARCH AREA:

NOTES
_____
_____
_____

HANDLER:
REWARD:

_____
_____
_____

MOOD:

_____
_____

WEATHER CONDITIONS:

PROBLEMS:

OVERALL EVALUATION

☆☆   ☺   😒
< 80%   50 - 80%   > 50% SUCCESS RATE

SCENT DETECTION TRAINING NO.

LOCATION: **DATE:**

TARGET SCENT:

PRIORITIES

SCENT ARTICLES:

HIDES:
NUMBER:

RESULTS

○ NOT CONTAMINATED
○ CONTAMINATED

SUCCESS:

SEARCH AREA:

NUMBER OF BLINDS:

NOTES

HANDLER:
REWARD:

WEATHER CONDITIONS:

MOOD:

PROBLEMS:

OVERALL EVALUATION

⭐ ☺ 😐
< 80%   50 – 80%   > 50% SUCCESS RATE

SCENT DETECTION TRAINING NO.

LOCATION: **DATE:**

TARGET SCENT:

HIDES:

NUMBER:

SUCCESS:

NUMBER OF BLINDS:

HANDLER:

REWARD:

MOOD:

PROBLEMS:

PRIORITIES

RESULTS

NOTES

OVERALL EVALUATION

- ⭐⭐   < 80%
- 🙂   50 – 80%
- 😐   > 50% SUCCESS RATE

SCENT ARTICLES:

○ NOT CONTAMINATED
○ CONTAMINATED

SEARCH AREA:

WEATHER CONDITIONS:

SCENT DETECTION TRAINING NO.

LOCATION: **DATE:**

TARGET SCENT:

PRIORITIES
_____
_____
_____
_____
_____

SCENT ARTICLES:

HIDES:
NUMBER:

RESULTS
_____
_____
_____
_____

○ NOT CONTAMINATED
○ CONTAMINATED

SUCCESS:

SEARCH AREA:

NUMBER OF BLINDS:

NOTES
_____
_____
_____
_____
_____
_____

HANDLER:
REWARD:

MOOD:

WEATHER CONDITIONS:

PROBLEMS:

OVERALL EVALUATION

⭐☺ ☺ 😐

< 80%   50 – 80%   > 50% SUCCESS RATE

SCENT DETECTION TRAINING NO.

LOCATION: **DATE:**

TARGET SCENT:

PRIORITIES
_____
_____
_____
_____

SCENT ARTICLES:

HIDES:
NUMBER:

RESULTS
_____
_____
_____
_____

○ NOT CONTAMINATED
○ CONTAMINATED

SUCCESS:

NUMBER OF BLINDS:

SEARCH AREA:

NOTES
_____
_____
_____
_____
_____
_____

HANDLER:
REWARD:

MOOD:

WEATHER CONDITIONS:

PROBLEMS:

OVERALL EVALUATION

☆☆   ☺   😐
< 80%   50 - 80%   > 50% SUCCESS RATE

SCENT DETECTION TRAINING NO.

LOCATION: **DATE:**

TARGET SCENT:

HIDES:
NUMBER:

SUCCESS:

NUMBER OF BLINDS:

HANDLER:
REWARD:

MOOD:

PROBLEMS:

PRIORITIES
_____
_____
_____
_____
_____

RESULTS
_____
_____
_____
_____
_____

NOTES
_____
_____
_____
_____
_____
_____
_____

OVERALL EVALUATION

☆☆   ☺   😐

< 80%   50 - 80%   > 50% SUCCESS RATE

SCENT ARTICLES:

○ NOT CONTAMINATED
○ CONTAMINATED

SEARCH AREA:

WEATHER CONDITIONS:

SCENT DETECTION TRAINING NO.

LOCATION: **DATE:**

TARGET SCENT:

PRIORITIES

SCENT ARTICLES:

HIDES:
NUMBER:

RESULTS

○ NOT CONTAMINATED
○ CONTAMINATED

SUCCESS:

NUMBER OF BLINDS:

SEARCH AREA:

NOTES

HANDLER:
REWARD:

MOOD:

WEATHER CONDITIONS:

PROBLEMS:

OVERALL EVALUATION

☆☆   ☺   😐
< 80%   50 - 80%   > 50% SUCCESS RATE

SCENT DETECTION TRAINING NO.

LOCATION: **DATE:**

TARGET SCENT:

HIDES:
NUMBER:

SUCCESS:

NUMBER OF BLINDS:

HANDLER:
REWARD:

MOOD:

PROBLEMS:

PRIORITIES
_____
_____
_____
_____
_____

RESULTS
_____
_____
_____
_____

NOTES
_____
_____
_____
_____
_____
_____
_____

OVERALL EVALUATION

⭐   🙂   😐

< 80%   50 – 80%   > 50% SUCCESS RATE

SCENT ARTICLES:

○ NOT CONTAMINATED
○ CONTAMINATED

SEARCH AREA:

WEATHER CONDITIONS:

SCENT DETECTION TRAINING NO.

LOCATION: **DATE:**

TARGET SCENT:

PRIORITIES

SCENT ARTICLES:

HIDES:
NUMBER:

RESULTS

○ NOT CONTAMINATED
○ CONTAMINATED

SUCCESS:

NUMBER OF BLINDS:

SEARCH AREA:

NOTES

HANDLER:
REWARD:

MOOD:

WEATHER CONDITIONS:

PROBLEMS:

OVERALL EVALUATION

< 80% | 50 - 80% | > 50% SUCCESS RATE

SCENT DETECTION TRAINING NO.

LOCATION: **DATE:**

TARGET SCENT:

PRIORITIES

SCENT ARTICLES:

○ NOT CONTAMINATED
○ CONTAMINATED

HIDES:
NUMBER:

RESULTS

SUCCESS:

SEARCH AREA:

NUMBER OF BLINDS:

NOTES

HANDLER:
REWARD:

WEATHER CONDITIONS:

MOOD:

PROBLEMS:

OVERALL EVALUATION

☆☺   ☺   😐
< 80%   50 - 80%   > 50% SUCCESS RATE

SCENT DETECTION TRAINING NO.

LOCATION: **DATE:**

TARGET SCENT:

PRIORITIES

SCENT ARTICLES:

HIDES:
NUMBER:

RESULTS

○ NOT CONTAMINATED
○ CONTAMINATED

SUCCESS:

NUMBER OF BLINDS:

SEARCH AREA:

NOTES

HANDLER:
REWARD:

MOOD:

WEATHER CONDITIONS:

PROBLEMS:

OVERALL EVALUATION

☆☆ ☺ 😐
< 80%   50 - 80%   > 50% SUCCESS RATE

SCENT DETECTION TRAINING NO.

LOCATION: **DATE:**

TARGET SCENT:

PRIORITIES

SCENT ARTICLES:

HIDES:

NUMBER:

RESULTS

○ NOT CONTAMINATED
○ CONTAMINATED

SUCCESS:

SEARCH AREA:

NUMBER OF BLINDS:

NOTES

HANDLER:

REWARD:

MOOD:

WEATHER CONDITIONS:

PROBLEMS:

OVERALL EVALUATION

< 80% | 50 – 80% | > 50% SUCCESS RATE

SCENT DETECTION TRAINING NO.

LOCATION: **DATE:**

TARGET SCENT:

PRIORITIES
_____
_____
_____
_____
_____

SCENT ARTICLES:

HIDES:
NUMBER:

RESULTS
_____
_____
_____
_____
_____

○ NOT CONTAMINATED
○ CONTAMINATED

SUCCESS:

NUMBER OF BLINDS:

SEARCH AREA:

NOTES
_____
_____
_____
_____

HANDLER:
REWARD:

_____
_____
_____

WEATHER CONDITIONS:

MOOD:

_____
_____

PROBLEMS:

OVERALL EVALUATION

☆☺   ☺   😐

< 80%   50 - 80%   > 50% SUCCESS RATE

SCENT DETECTION TRAINING NO.

LOCATION: **DATE:**

TARGET SCENT:

PRIORITIES
_____
_____
_____
_____
_____

SCENT ARTICLES:

HIDES:
NUMBER:

RESULTS
_____
_____
_____
_____
_____
_____

○ NOT CONTAMINATED
○ CONTAMINATED

SUCCESS:

SEARCH AREA:

NUMBER OF BLINDS:

NOTES
_____
_____
_____
_____

HANDLER:
REWARD:

_____
_____
_____

WEATHER CONDITIONS:

MOOD:

PROBLEMS:

OVERALL EVALUATION

⭐☺ ☺ 😐
< 80%   50 - 80%   > 50% SUCCESS RATE

SCENT DETECTION TRAINING NO.

LOCATION: **DATE:**

TARGET SCENT:

PRIORITIES

SCENT ARTICLES:

HIDES:
NUMBER:

RESULTS

○ NOT CONTAMINATED
○ CONTAMINATED

SUCCESS:

NUMBER OF BLINDS:

SEARCH AREA:

NOTES

HANDLER:
REWARD:

MOOD:

WEATHER CONDITIONS:

PROBLEMS:

OVERALL EVALUATION

☆☆ ☺ 😐
< 80%   50 - 80%   > 50% SUCCESS RATE

SCENT DETECTION TRAINING NO.

LOCATION: **DATE:**

TARGET SCENT:

PRIORITIES
_____
_____
_____
_____
_____

SCENT ARTICLES:

HIDES:

NUMBER:

RESULTS
_____
_____
_____
_____
_____

○ NOT CONTAMINATED
○ CONTAMINATED

SUCCESS:

NUMBER OF BLINDS:

SEARCH AREA:

NOTES
_____
_____
_____
_____
_____
_____
_____
_____
_____

HANDLER:

REWARD:

MOOD:

WEATHER CONDITIONS:

PROBLEMS:

OVERALL EVALUATION

⭐⭐   ☺   😐

< 80%   50 - 80%   > 50% SUCCESS RATE

SCENT DETECTION TRAINING NO.

LOCATION: **DATE:**

TARGET SCENT:

PRIORITIES

SCENT ARTICLES:

HIDES:
NUMBER:

RESULTS

○ NOT CONTAMINATED
○ CONTAMINATED

SUCCESS:

NUMBER OF BLINDS:

SEARCH AREA:

NOTES

HANDLER:
REWARD:

MOOD:

WEATHER CONDITIONS:

PROBLEMS:

OVERALL EVALUATION

☆☆   ☺   😒

< 80%   50 - 80%   > 50% SUCCESS RATE

SCENT DETECTION TRAINING NO.

LOCATION: **DATE:**

TARGET SCENT:

PRIORITIES
_____
_____
_____
_____

SCENT ARTICLES:

○ NOT CONTAMINATED
○ CONTAMINATED

HIDES:
NUMBER:

RESULTS
_____
_____
_____
_____

SUCCESS:

SEARCH AREA:

NUMBER OF BLINDS:

NOTES
_____
_____
_____
_____
_____
_____
_____

HANDLER:
REWARD:

WEATHER CONDITIONS:

MOOD:

PROBLEMS:

OVERALL EVALUATION

  ☆☆   ☺   😐

 < 80%   50 - 80%   > 50% SUCCESS RATE

SCENT DETECTION TRAINING NO.

LOCATION: **DATE:**

TARGET SCENT:

PRIORITIES

SCENT ARTICLES:

HIDES:

NUMBER:

RESULTS

◯ NOT CONTAMINATED
◯ CONTAMINATED

SUCCESS:

NUMBER OF BLINDS:

SEARCH AREA:

NOTES

HANDLER:

REWARD:

MOOD:

WEATHER CONDITIONS:

PROBLEMS:

OVERALL EVALUATION

☆☆   ☺   😐

< 80%   50 - 80%   > 50% SUCCESS RATE

SCENT DETECTION TRAINING NO.

LOCATION: **DATE:**

TARGET SCENT:

PRIORITIES

SCENT ARTICLES:

○ NOT CONTAMINATED
○ CONTAMINATED

HIDES:

NUMBER:

RESULTS

SUCCESS:

NUMBER OF BLINDS:

SEARCH AREA:

NOTES

HANDLER:

REWARD:

MOOD:

WEATHER CONDITIONS:

PROBLEMS:

OVERALL EVALUATION

< 80%   50 - 80%   > 50% SUCCESS RATE

SCENT DETECTION TRAINING NO.

LOCATION: **DATE:**

TARGET SCENT:

PRIORITIES

SCENT ARTICLES:

HIDES:
NUMBER:

RESULTS

○ NOT CONTAMINATED
○ CONTAMINATED

SUCCESS:

NUMBER OF BLINDS:

SEARCH AREA:

NOTES

HANDLER:
REWARD:

MOOD:

WEATHER CONDITIONS:

PROBLEMS:

OVERALL EVALUATION

☆☆   ☺   😒

< 80%   50 - 80%   > 50% SUCCESS RATE

SCENT DETECTION TRAINING NO.

LOCATION: **DATE:**

TARGET SCENT:

PRIORITIES
_____
_____
_____
_____
_____

SCENT ARTICLES:

HIDES:
NUMBER:

RESULTS
_____
_____
_____
_____
_____

○ NOT CONTAMINATED
○ CONTAMINATED

SUCCESS:

NUMBER OF BLINDS:

NOTES
_____
_____
_____
_____
_____
_____
_____
_____

SEARCH AREA:

HANDLER:
REWARD:

MOOD:

WEATHER CONDITIONS:

PROBLEMS:

OVERALL EVALUATION

☆☆ 🙂 😐
< 80% 50 - 80% > 50% SUCCESS RATE

SCENT DETECTION TRAINING NO.

LOCATION: **DATE:**

TARGET SCENT:

PRIORITIES

SCENT ARTICLES:

HIDES:
NUMBER:

RESULTS

○ NOT CONTAMINATED
○ CONTAMINATED

SUCCESS:

NUMBER OF BLINDS:

SEARCH AREA:

NOTES

HANDLER:
REWARD:

MOOD:

WEATHER CONDITIONS:

PROBLEMS:

OVERALL EVALUATION

< 80%   50 - 80%   > 50% SUCCESS RATE

SCENT DETECTION TRAINING NO.

LOCATION: **DATE:**

TARGET SCENT:

PRIORITIES

SCENT ARTICLES:

HIDES:
NUMBER:

RESULTS

○ NOT CONTAMINATED
○ CONTAMINATED

SUCCESS:

SEARCH AREA:

NUMBER OF BLINDS:

NOTES

HANDLER:
REWARD:

MOOD:

WEATHER CONDITIONS:

PROBLEMS:

OVERALL EVALUATION

☆☆   ☺   😐
< 80%   50 - 80%   > 50% SUCCESS RATE

SCENT DETECTION TRAINING NO.

LOCATION: **DATE:**

TARGET SCENT:

PRIORITIES

SCENT ARTICLES:

HIDES:
NUMBER:

RESULTS

◯ NOT CONTAMINATED
◯ CONTAMINATED

SUCCESS:

NUMBER OF BLINDS:

SEARCH AREA:

NOTES

HANDLER:
REWARD:

MOOD:

WEATHER CONDITIONS:

PROBLEMS:

OVERALL EVALUATION

⭐⭐   ☺   😐

< 80%   50 - 80%   > 50% SUCCESS RATE

SCENT DETECTION TRAINING NO.

LOCATION: **DATE:**

TARGET SCENT:

PRIORITIES

SCENT ARTICLES:

HIDES:
NUMBER:

RESULTS

○ NOT CONTAMINATED
○ CONTAMINATED

SUCCESS:

SEARCH AREA:

NUMBER OF BLINDS:

NOTES

HANDLER:
REWARD:

WEATHER CONDITIONS:

MOOD:

PROBLEMS:

OVERALL EVALUATION

< 80%   50 - 80%   > 50% SUCCESS RATE

SCENT DETECTION TRAINING NO.

LOCATION: **DATE:**

TARGET SCENT:

HIDES:
- NUMBER:
- SUCCESS:
- NUMBER OF BLINDS:

HANDLER:
- REWARD:
- MOOD:
- PROBLEMS:

PRIORITIES

RESULTS

NOTES

OVERALL EVALUATION

⭐⭐   🙂   😐

< 80%   50 - 80%   > 50% SUCCESS RATE

SCENT ARTICLES:

○ NOT CONTAMINATED
○ CONTAMINATED

SEARCH AREA:

WEATHER CONDITIONS:

SCENT DETECTION TRAINING NO.

LOCATION: **DATE:**

TARGET SCENT:

PRIORITIES
_____
_____
_____
_____
_____

SCENT ARTICLES:

HIDES:
NUMBER:

RESULTS
_____
_____
_____
_____

○ NOT CONTAMINATED
○ CONTAMINATED

SUCCESS:

NUMBER OF BLINDS:

SEARCH AREA:

NOTES
_____
_____
_____
_____
_____
_____
_____
_____

HANDLER:
REWARD:

MOOD:

WEATHER CONDITIONS:

PROBLEMS:

OVERALL EVALUATION

☆☆ ☺ 😐
< 80% 50 - 80% > 50% SUCCESS RATE

SCENT DETECTION TRAINING NO.

LOCATION: **DATE:**

TARGET SCENT:

PRIORITIES
_____
_____
_____
_____
_____
_____

SCENT ARTICLES:

HIDES:

NUMBER:

RESULTS
_____
_____
_____
_____

○ NOT CONTAMINATED
○ CONTAMINATED

SUCCESS:

NUMBER OF BLINDS:

SEARCH AREA:

NOTES
_____
_____
_____
_____
_____
_____
_____
_____

HANDLER:

REWARD:

MOOD:

WEATHER CONDITIONS:

PROBLEMS:

OVERALL EVALUATION

⭐ 😊 😐
< 80%   50 - 80%   > 50% SUCCESS RATE

SCENT DETECTION TRAINING NO.

LOCATION: **DATE:**

TARGET SCENT:

PRIORITIES

SCENT ARTICLES:

HIDES:
NUMBER:

RESULTS

○ NOT CONTAMINATED
○ CONTAMINATED

SUCCESS:

SEARCH AREA:

NUMBER OF BLINDS:

NOTES

HANDLER:
REWARD:

MOOD:

WEATHER CONDITIONS:

PROBLEMS:

OVERALL EVALUATION

< 80% | 50 – 80% | > 50% SUCCESS RATE

SCENT DETECTION TRAINING NO.

LOCATION: **DATE:**

TARGET SCENT:

PRIORITIES
_____
_____
_____
_____
_____

SCENT ARTICLES:

HIDES:

NUMBER:

RESULTS
_____
_____
_____
_____

○ NOT CONTAMINATED
○ CONTAMINATED

SUCCESS:

NUMBER OF BLINDS:

SEARCH AREA:

NOTES
_____
_____
_____
_____
_____
_____
_____
_____

HANDLER:

REWARD:

MOOD:

WEATHER CONDITIONS:

PROBLEMS:

OVERALL EVALUATION

⭐☆   🙂   😕

< 80%   50 - 80%   > 50% SUCCESS RATE

SCENT DETECTION TRAINING NO.

LOCATION: **DATE:**

TARGET SCENT:

PRIORITIES

SCENT ARTICLES:

HIDES:
NUMBER:

RESULTS

○ NOT CONTAMINATED
○ CONTAMINATED

SUCCESS:

NUMBER OF BLINDS:

SEARCH AREA:

NOTES

HANDLER:
REWARD:

MOOD:

WEATHER CONDITIONS:

PROBLEMS:

OVERALL EVALUATION

< 80%   50 - 80%   > 50% SUCCESS RATE

SCENT DETECTION TRAINING NO.

LOCATION: **DATE:**

TARGET SCENT:

PRIORITIES
_____
_____
_____
_____
_____

SCENT ARTICLES:

HIDES:

NUMBER:

RESULTS
_____
_____
_____
_____
_____

○ NOT CONTAMINATED
○ CONTAMINATED

SUCCESS:

NUMBER OF BLINDS:

SEARCH AREA:

NOTES
_____
_____
_____

HANDLER:

REWARD:

_____
_____
_____
_____

MOOD:

_____
_____

WEATHER CONDITIONS:

PROBLEMS:

OVERALL EVALUATION

☆☆   ☺   😐

< 80%   50 - 80%   > 50% SUCCESS RATE

SCENT DETECTION TRAINING NO.

LOCATION: **DATE:**

TARGET SCENT:

PRIORITIES
_____
_____
_____
_____
_____

SCENT ARTICLES:

○ NOT CONTAMINATED
○ CONTAMINATED

HIDES:

NUMBER:

RESULTS
_____
_____
_____
_____
_____

SUCCESS:

NUMBER OF BLINDS:

SEARCH AREA:

NOTES
_____
_____
_____

HANDLER:

REWARD:

_____
_____
_____

MOOD:

_____
_____

WEATHER CONDITIONS:

PROBLEMS:

OVERALL EVALUATION

☆☺ ☺ 😐

< 80%   50 - 80%   > 50% SUCCESS RATE

HIDES:

NUMBER:

SUCCESS:

NUMBER OF BLINDS:

HANDLER:

REWARD:

MOOD:

PROBLEMS:

RESULTS

NOTES

OVERALL EVALUATION

< 80%   50 - 80%   > 50% SUCCESS

HIDES:

NUMBER:

SUCCESS:

NUMBER OF BLINDS:

HANDLER:

REWARD:

MOOD:

PROBLEMS:

RESULTS

NOTES

OVERALL EVALUATION

< 80%   50 - 80%   > 50% SUCCESS RATE

HIDES:

NUMBER:

SUCCESS:

NUMBER OF BLINDS:

HANDLER:

REWARD:

MOOD:

PROBLEMS:

RESULTS

NOTES

OVERALL EVALUATION

< 80%   50 - 80%   > 50% SUCCESS

HIDES:

NUMBER:

SUCCESS:

NUMBER OF BLINDS:

HANDLER:

REWARD:

MOOD:

PROBLEMS:

RESULTS

NOTES

OVERALL EVALUATION

< 80%   50 - 80%   > 50% SUCCESS RATE

HIDES:

NUMBER:

SUCCESS:

NUMBER OF BLINDS:

HANDLER:

REWARD:

MOOD:

PROBLEMS:

RESULTS

NOTES

OVERALL EVALUATION

< 80%   50 - 80%   > 50% SUCCESS

HIDES:

NUMBER:

SUCCESS:

NUMBER OF BLINDS:

HANDLER:

REWARD:

MOOD:

PROBLEMS:

RESULTS

NOTES

OVERALL EVALUATION

< 80%   50 - 80%   > 50% SUCCESS RA

HIDES:

NUMBER:

SUCCESS:

NUMBER OF BLINDS:

HANDLER:

REWARD:

MOOD:

PROBLEMS:

RESULTS

NOTES

OVERALL EVALUATION

< 80%   50 - 80%   > 50% SUCCESS

HIDES:

NUMBER:

SUCCESS:

NUMBER OF BLINDS:

HANDLER:

REWARD:

MOOD:

PROBLEMS:

RESULTS

NOTES

OVERALL EVALUATION

< 80%   50 - 80%   > 50% SUCCESS RATE

NOTES

Manufactured by Amazon.ca
Bolton, ON